The
Counsels
of Cormac

Thomas Cleary

D O U B L E D A Y

NEW YORK   LONDON
TORONTO
SYDNEY   AUCKLAND

The
Counsels
of Cormac

AN ANCIENT IRISH
GUIDE TO LEADERSHIP

———

A NEW TRANSLATION
FROM THE
ORIGINAL OLD IRISH

PUBLISHED BY DOUBLEDAY
a division of Random House, Inc.

DOUBLEDAY and the portrayal of an anchor with a dolphin are
registered trademarks of Random House, Inc.

Book design by Maria Carella

Library of Congress Cataloging-in-Publication Data
Tecosca Cormaic.
The counsels of Cormac : An ancient Irish guide to leadership /
Thomas Cleary. — 1st ed.
p. cm.
Attributed to Cormac Mac Airt.
ISBN 0-385-51313-5 (alk. paper)
I. Maxims, Irish—Translations into English. 2. Proverbs, Irish—Translations
into English. 3. Kings and rulers—Duties—Early works to 1800. 4. Cormac
Mac Airt, King of Ireland, fl. 227–260. I. Cormac Mac Airt, King of Ireland,
fl. 227–260. II. Cleary, Thomas F., 1949– III. Title.
PB1421.T43 2004
398.9'9162—dc22   2004041317

PRINTED IN THE UNITED STATES OF AMERICA

October 2004

First Edition

10 9 8 7 6 5 4 3 2 1

INTRODUCTION

Saruigheann eagnacht gach saidhbhreas.
WISDOM IS BETTER THAN ANY WEALTH.

Irish traditions honoring wisdom are as old as Celtic
mythology, the ancient roots of which reach back into
high antiquity. Following a cultural heritage originating
from the same source as the Hindu civilization of India,
in their ancient lore the Celtic peoples of Ireland
traditionally claimed Asiatic origins and maintained
legends of contact and cooperation with other great
cultures of antiquity, including the Minoan, Egyptian,
Greek, and Hebrew cultures, in their immemorial
journeys to the West.

Knowledge was highly valued in the thinking of the Celts,
as among the other peoples of old with whom they were
associated through history and myth. The range of
knowledge pursued by the Celts, moreover, extended from
understanding of the ordinary and the everyday to
experience of the extraordinary and the inexplicable.
From herding and farming to science and philosophy to
enchantment and mystical vision, the continuum of
Celtic culture encompassed a wide range of human

concerns, from the most mundane matters to remarkably sublime metaphysics.

The original leaders of all the Celtic peoples, according to Irish tradition, were not professional warriors but experts in the arts and sciences. The Gaelic word *fodhla*, meaning wisdom, is a mythopoetic name of Ireland itself; the legendary king Ollamh Fodhla, the multitalented Doctor of Wisdom, is one of the most important figures of Irish mythology.

According to legend, Ollamh Fodhla initiated a new order in Ireland more than three thousand years ago, absorbing the high arts of the earlier Celtic culture, codifying the laws, and organizing a more integrated sociopolitical structure. Pictured as a master of all branches of knowledge, the Doctor of Wisdom is credited with founding a school of learning and a parliament of kings, two of the central institutions of the original Irish civilization.

Education in the broadest sense was central to Irish Celtic culture, and public schools derived from the original Druidical tradition continued to thrive in Ireland for more than a thousand years after the establishment of Christian institutions. In these native schools the ancient lore of Celtic Ireland was transmitted, including the highly sophisticated disciplines of medicine, law, literature, and history.

These schools were also receptive to outside input as they evolved internally over the ages. In addition to legends of contact with the school of Alexandria in Egypt and Buddhist missionaries from India, the Irish literature of the Middle Ages evinces active intellectual interchange with contemporary continental cultures.

The Irish parliament of kings, the celebrated Feis of Tara, was a triennial congress of chieftains, held under the auspices of the high king at the spiritual center of pagan Ireland. This parliament of kings was the occasion of a great national fair. There were also local parliaments and fairs, held at intervals all over Ireland. Integrating diplomatic, social, legal, and commercial functions, the parliaments and their associated fairs were essential organs of Irish culture.

The kings of Celtic Ireland, great and small, were elected by the freeholders of their territories. As there was no primogeniture and kingship was not hereditary, the personal qualities of candidates for kingship were paramount. Thus one of the functions of education in

Celtic Ireland was the cultivation of people capable of kingship, acquainting them with knowledge of all the branches of learning. The Old Irish *Tecosca Cormaic*, or *Counsels of Cormac*, is one of the best-known surviving classics of this tradition.

Cormac MacAirt (circa 227–260 CE), to whom these counsels are attributed, is traditionally portrayed by Irish poets and historians as among the greatest of the Irish high kings. He is referred to in the *Counsels* as "Cormac, Grandson of Conn," after his grandfather Conn Cetlach, or Conn of the Hundred Battles, who was also a famous high king in the third century CE.

Conn was known mainly for military prowess and was immortalized in Irish annals for wresting the high kingship from a would-be tyrant who deviated from ancient custom by trying to establish his own heirs in hereditary control over Ireland. In contrast to Conn's martial reputation, King Cormac is famed for achievements in culture and civilization.

Cormac's tenure as high king is renowned in Irish lore for peace, prosperity, and justice. He is considered to have maintained the largest retinue of any of the high kings of Ireland, including a diverse group of clients from among the Gauls, Romans, Franks, Frisians, Lombards, Caledonians, Saxons, and Cruthin or Picts. Cormac is said to have gathered chroniclers from all over Ireland to compile a unified body of historical and political lore, which included the deeds, rights, and duties of kings.

King Cormac is also reputed to have authored several works himself. These include a book on the principles of criminal law and a collection of ancient historical and genealogical information, as well as the handbook translated here, *The Counsels of Cormac*, his famous manual of practical and moral instructions for leaders.

THE COUNSELS OF CORMAC

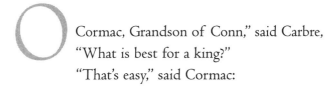

"O Cormac, Grandson of Conn," said Carbre,
"What is best for a king?"
"That's easy," said Cormac:

Composure rather than wrath,
Patience rather than contention,
Geniality rather than arrogance.

Attention to tradition,
True reciprocity,
Hostages in custody.

Military action for just cause,
Justice without bloodshed,
Leniency within the integrity of the law.

Goodwill to tribes,
Distinct guarantees,
Just judgments,
Fasting against neighboring territories.

Glorifying the sacred,
Respecting poets,
Adoration of God.

Productivity in his reign,

Attention to every unfortunate,
Many charities.

Fruit on trees,
Fish in estuaries,
Fertile land.

Ships invited into port,
Goods imported from overseas,
Appropriation of things cast up by the sea.

Silk clothing,
A hand wielding swords in defense of every
    tribe,
Attacks across borders.

Let him visit the ailing,
Let him improve the condition of the
    indigent.

Let him have legitimate claim to truth,
Let him rebuke falsehood.

Let him love justice,
Let him quell fear.

Let him destroy criminals,
Let him bring just pronouncements,
Let him support every branch of learning.

Let him purchase what is valuable,
Let him improve what is worthless,
Let him have abundant wine and mead.

Let him knit every peace treaty together,
Let him declare every clear judgment,
Let him speak every truth.

"For it is through the truth of the chieftain
    that God gives all that."

O Cormac, Grandson of Conn," said Carbre,
"What is the proper authority of kingship?"
"That's easy. The authority that rules over a
stable land I have and will give back to
you," said Cormac to Carbre:

Let him contain the powerful,
Let him execute the evil,
Let him foster the good.

Let him subdue outlaws,
Let him stop robbery and theft,
Let him establish order in relations.

Let him contract peace treaties,
Let him establish law,
Let him correct injustice and punish illegal acts.

Let him sentence criminals,
Let him free the innocent,

Let him protect the righteous,
Let him constrain the unrighteous.

Let him warn outlaws:
Full liability for everyone responsible,

The whole penalties for accessories with knowledge,
Half penalties for those without knowledge.

With the dignity of a king
And the prerogatives of a chieftain,
Let him maintain the integrity of the right
    proper to every man
Of what is his of sea and land
With rightful properties for the tribes that are
    his.

In regard to crimes of hand,
Goings about of feet,
What the eyes look at,
Misdeeds of speech,
What the ears listen to,
With true facts in confidence
He clarifies and attends to the right of every
    chief:
Let him bring every one together under law.

"These are the legal prescriptions, the rights
    and duties, of a chieftain in respect to
    tribes."

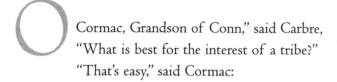 Cormac, Grandson of Conn," said Carbre,
"What is best for the interest of a tribe?"
"That's easy," said Cormac:

Gathering of good people,
Frequent conferences,
An inquiring mind.

Consulting the wise,
Destroying every evil,
Bringing about every good.

A regular court,
Following traditions,
A legal assembly.

Administration of law by the chieftain,
Just leadership,
Not oppressing the wretched.

Protection of amity,
Leniency toward those of good morals,
Consolidating relationship.

Piecing together related information,
Carrying out administration of government,

Authority of ancient alliances.

Treaty of friendship without cancellation,
Militia without vainglory,
Sternness toward enemies, innocence toward
    kin.

Generous pledges, complete repayment, just
    rulings;
Honest witnesses, contracts without fraud,
    interest on loss;
Equivalence of contractual obligations,
    seasonal lending, pledges according to
    statuses.

Wholesome lending, loans for proper
    purposes;
An equivalent for every good;
Dignified response, permissible measure.

Study of each art,
Knowledge of each technical vocabulary,
Diversified skills in crafts.

Argumentation using legal precedents,
Pronouncement with legal maxims,

Giving alms, justice, and mercy to the poor.

Sureties against judgments,
Honest contracts.
Listening to the venerable, deafness to
common fools.

"Let him not be lax about the interest of the
tribe, let him not be greasy in the banquet
hall—this is best for the interest of the
tribe."

Cormac, Grandson of Conn," said Carbre,
"What are things fitting for a chieftain and an
alehouse?"
"That's easy," said Cormac:

Composure in the company of a good chief,
Brilliance of lanterns,
Effort for the multitude,
Arranging the seating.

Generosity of dispensers,
Quickness at dispensing,
Readiness of supply.

Consideration for the chief,
Temperance of high spirits,
Brevity of storytelling.

A cheerful face,
Welcome to poets,
Silence during a poem,
Melodious music.

"This is fitting for a chieftain and an
alehouse," said Cormac to Carbre.

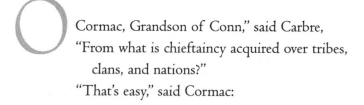

"O Cormac, Grandson of Conn," said Carbre,
"From what is chieftaincy acquired over tribes,
    clans, and nations?"
"That's easy," said Cormac:

It is gained by excellence
Of appearance, tribe, and discernment;
Wisdom, dignity, and generosity;
Heredity, integrity, and eloquence;
Warding off outlaws and having many friends.

What are the traditional prescriptions for a chieftain?" said Carbre.

"That's easy," said Cormac:

Let him be well-controlled,
Let him be sober,
Let him be proactive.

Let him be of goodwill,
Let him be affable,
Let him be humble.

Let him be high-minded,
Let him be quick,
Let him be firm.

Let him be a poet,
Let him be a traditionalist,
Let him be wise.

Let him be generous,
Let him be genial,
Let him be tender.

Let him be strict,
Let him be caring,

Let him be compassionate.

Let him be just,
Let him be perceptive,
Let him be constant.

Let him be forbearing,
Let him be abstemious,
Let him uplift those disabled by indigence.

Let him deliver just judgments,
Let him feed every orphan,
Let him destroy every bad example.

Let him hate falsehood, let him love truth;
Let him be mindless of malevolence, let him
    be mindful of kindness;
Let him be accompanied at conventions, let
    him be alone at secret councils.

Let him be brilliant in company,
Let him be the sun of the banquet hall,
Let him be host of conventions and
    congresses.

Let him be a lover of knowledge and wisdom,
Let him be a constrainer of evil,
Let him be administrator of punishment to
    everyone who is undutiful.

Let him entertain each individual according to
    his right,
Let him give each individual his due,
Let him be a judge of each individual
    according to his status,
Let him be a benefactor of each individual
    according to his professional degree and
    according to his skill.

Let his pledges be sure,
Let his enforcement be lenient,
Let his judgments and decisions be incisive
    and not ponderous.

"For it is by these traditional prescriptions
    that kings and chieftains are judged," said
    Cormac to Carbre.

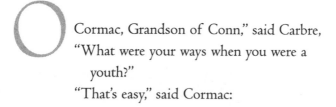

"Cormac, Grandson of Conn," said Carbre, "What were your ways when you were a youth?"

"That's easy," said Cormac:

I was one who listened to the woods;
I was one who watched the stars;
I was one who was blind to mysteries.

I was silent in the wilderness, talkative in society;
I was genial in the banquet hall, troublesome in combat;
I was quick to stand watch, I was kind in friendship.

I was a healer of the sick,
I was gentle to the feeble,
I was strong against the powerful.

I was not harsh, so as not to be satirized;
I was not pliant, so as not to be servile;
I wasn't clinging, so as not to be a burden;
I was not loquacious, even if intelligent;
I was not aggressive, even though strong;
I was not daring, even though quick.

I didn't ridicule the old, though I was young;
I wasn't arrogant, though I was dominant;
I would not talk about anyone in his absence;
I would not ask but would give.

"For it is through these practices that a youth
may harden so as to become mature and a
regal warrior."

O Cormac, Grandson of Conn," said Carbre, "What were your exploits when you were a youth?"

"That's easy," said Cormac:

I would kill a boar and follow tracks when I was alone;
I would march against a band of five when I was in a band of five.
I was ready to kill when I was in a band of ten;
I was ready to plunder when I was in a band of twenty;
I was ready to battle when I was in a band of a hundred.

"These were my exploits," said Cormac.

Cormac, Grandson of Conn," said Carbre,
"What is worst, to you, that you've seen?"
"That's easy," said Cormac. "Faces of enemies
on a battleground."

 Cormac, Grandson of Conn," said Carbre,
"What is most pleasing to you that you've
heard?"
"That's easy," said Cormac:

A cheer after victory,
Praise after reward,
The invitation of a fine lady to adore her.

O Cormac, Grandson of Conn," said Carbre, "What is best for me?"

"That's easy," said Cormac: "If you heed my advice, you would not give your honor for ale or for food, as protection of reputation is better than assurance of food."

Don't be proud unless you're a homesteader.
Don't keep mares without stallions.
Don't give feasts without ale.
Don't use a lot of milk if you have no cattle.
Don't dress up if you have no sheep.
For it is wrong in the courts of the world
To be proud without producing,
To indulge in wanton luxury without horses,
To entertain without ale,
To be prodigal with dairy products without raising cattle,
To dress up without raising sheep.

O Cormac, Grandson of Conn," said Carbre,
"What is good for me?"
"That's easy," said Cormac, "if you heed my
advice:"

Don't ridicule the elderly, though you be
young;
Nor the poor, though you be rich;
Nor the ragged, though you be wealthy;
Nor the lame, though you be fleet;
Nor the blind, though you can see;
Nor the weak, though you be strong;
Nor the senseless, though you be prudent;
Nor the foolish, though you be wise.

Don't be sluggish, don't be irascible;
Don't be slothful, don't be stingy;
Don't be idle, don't be jealous.

"For everyone who is sluggish, irascible,
slothful, stingy, idle, and jealous is
repugnant to God and society."

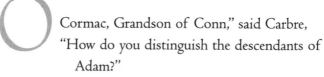

Cormac, Grandson of Conn," said Carbre,
"How do you distinguish the descendants of
Adam?"
"That's easy," said Cormac. "I get to know
them all—men and women, sons and
daughters, and in general."
"How is that?" asked Carbre.
Cormac said:

One who is imperturbable is wise,
One who is honorable is just,
One who is patient is constant.

One who is studious is well-informed,
One who loves family is forbearing,
One who is healthy is cheerful.

One who is rash is a laughingstock,
One who is enslaved is gloomy,
One who is poor is proud.

One who is ignorant is quarrelsome,
One who is unwise is shameless,
One who is fearful is timid.

One who is weak from illness is frank,

One who is ugly is nurturing,
One who is afflicted is anxious.

One who is fearful is cautious,
One who causes fear is cruel,
One who is indigent will cheat.

One who's contentious is often in court,
One who's aggressive is fond of hounds and
    hunting,
One who's in love is often in bed.

A landholder is rich,
A carpenter is versatile,
A sophisticate is liberal.

A satirist is poison,
An anxious person is hasty,
A lie is bitter, a truth is sweet.

Artistic women are sweet-mouthed,
Bad women are promiscuous,
Their sons are trouble, a sorrow to him who
    has them.

Cormac, Grandson of Conn," said Carbre,
"How many ways of acquiring incapacity are
 there?"
"That's easy," said Cormac:

Swearing after a legal ruling,
Hasty decisions,
Arousal of anger.

Lying whispering,
Impugning truth,
Forswearing a house of prayer.

Recanting judgments,
Lamentation at a feast,
A lying chief.

Laughing at the elderly,
Concealing historical fact,
Playing on a cliff.

Shooting without aim,
Competition with a fool,
Arrogance toward a king.

Failure to fulfill the law,

Performance of anything evil,
Wronging friends.

Promiscuity,
Taking a shine to every novelty,
Being hostile to everything customary.

Action without evidence,
Weakness as a custodian,
Paying for legal decisions.

Being without a way of life,
Lending a lot, a multitude of friends;
Lamenting to a king, talking a lot without
    making sense.

"That is acquisition of incapacity," said
    Cormac.

Wisdom deserves honor
Intelligence overcomes fury,
A doubter is opinionated.

One who is loving is sorrowful,
One who is sickly is cantankerous,
One who is deceitful is contentious.

A fool is dangerous,
A boaster is unguarded,
One who is violent is oppressive.

A homesteader is careful,
A bad warrior is furious,
An obsessive is shameless.

A danger is dreadful,
A darkness is awful,
A rent payer is low in status.

An idler is corpulent,
A wretch is shameless,
A culprit is fearful.

One who is abusive is frustrated,
One who is fearful is timid,

One who is evil-tongued is contentious.

One who is wanton is fiery,
A good tribe is populous,
A good king is a defender.

One who is litigious is a grumbler,
One who is courageous is gentle,
One who is violent is negligent.

One who tells the future is lying,
One who is wasteful is arrogant,
One who is impatient is ridiculous.

One who is powerful is abusive,
One who is insulting is overbearing,
One who is sensible is moderate.

A chronicler is a good advisor,
One who is unruly is a coward,
One who is well disciplined is a sage.

One who is honest acknowledges rights,
A good skill is productive,
One who is poor is humane.

O Cormac, Grandson of Conn," said Carbre,
"How do you interpret weathers?"
"That's easy," said Cormac:

Ice is mother to grain,
Snow is father to bacon,
Wet is a portent of feud,
Drought is a portent of plague.
Difficult in straits is wind,
Best of weathers is mist,
Better his brother rain.
Thunder's not fruitful,
Except for the sea.

O Cormac, Grandson of Conn," said Carbre,
"What is the worst husbandry?"
"That's easy. Husbandry by which neither
dignity nor life are obtained. There is
another husbandry that's even worse: *Get!*
Give! Bring! Hand over!"

Warning of Cormac to Carbre:

Don't threaten a king,
Don't join up with a fool,
Don't associate with a freebooter,
Don't consort with a criminal.

Don't buy from six unqualified persons
    according to the Irish learned:
from a housewife,
from a drunk,
from a moron,
from a madman,
from a noble,
from a blind person.

Don't go against a chariot,
or a throw,
or a hill,
or a large expanse of water,
or a hazard,
or a spear.

Don't join in slander,
Don't be a fool in an assembly,
Don't be sad in an alehouse.

Don't be forgetful of an agreement,
Don't be intractable,
Don't be one who quarrels with truth.

Don't be smart at lying.
Don't be flunky to a thief,
Don't be conflict's chief.

Don't be a thicket of strife,
Don't lend your words to everyone,
Don't promise what you don't have.

Don't be a spendthrift, so you won't be in
    debt;
Don't be aggressive, so you won't be disgraced;
Don't be contentious, so you won't be disliked.

Don't be quarrelsome, so you don't get your
    head broken;
Don't be rough, so you won't be uncouth;
Don't be combative, so you won't lose your
    head.

Don't live away from your land, so you won't
    be negligent;
Don't be harsh, so you won't be rude;

Don't be too bountiful, so you won't suffer
decline.

Don't be lazy, so you won't be ineffective;
Don't be overeager, so you won't be a fool;
Don't be contentious, so you won't be isolated.

Don't be a guarantor of anyone so you won't
be useless to neighbors.

O Cormac, Grandson of Conn," said Carbre,
"What is lasting in the world?"
"That's easy," said Cormac. "Grass, bronze,
yew wood."

Cormac, Grandson of Conn," said Carbre,
"What is worst for the human body?"
"That's easy," said Cormac:

Sitting too much,
Reclining too much,
Prolonged inactivity,
Heavy lifting,
Overexertion,
Alienation from society.
Running too much,
Jumping too much,
Stumbling often,
Leg over the bed rail,
Fast riding,
Gazing at fire,
Stepping blind in the dark,
Wax,
Cow colostrum,
New ale,
Bull meat,
Curdled milk,
Dry food,
Bog water,
Early rising,
Cold,

Sun,
Hunger,
Excessive drinking,
Excessive eating,
Excessive sleeping,
Excessive peccadilloes,
Loneliness and melancholy,
Running uphill,
Calling into the wind,
A blow beyond one's capacity,
Drying out by the fire,
Summer dew,
Winter dew,
Beating ashes or dust,
Swimming after eating one's fill,
Sleeping supine,
A big drink,
Frenzy,
Foolishness.

Cormac, Grandson of Conn," said Carbre,
"What is the worst argumentation and
   discourse?"
"That's easy," said Cormac. "There are
   seventeen characteristics of bad
   argumentation."

Contention against knowledge,
Resort to bad language,
A multitude of insults,
Contention without proof.

Prolixity or sluggishness of speech,
Talking at the same time as another,
Intellectual hair-splitting,
Unestablished proof.

Spurning books,
Turning against tradition,
Talking too loud,
Flightiness of argument.

Rebuking the multitude,
Fighting everyone,
Pompous vanity,

Screaming,
Swearing after judgment is pronounced.

O Cormac, Grandson of Conn," said Carbre,
"What is the worst discourse?"
"That's easy," said Cormac. "When it is
incompetent and forgetful."

O Cormac, Grandson of Conn," said Carbre,
"What is the worst plea?"
"That's easy," said Cormac. "A contentious
plea; a flimsy, slow, prolix plea."

O Cormac, Grandson of Conn," said Carbre,
"What is the worst plea in court?"
"That's easy," said Cormac:

An angry, importunate, long-winded plea;
A flighty, uncertain plea;
An empty, venting suit.

Rapid, forgetful argumentation;
Inciting anger;
Oppressive wrath.

Liability to err through partiality;
Swearing hasty, reckless oaths;
Loud, vociferous response.

Disturbing the court;
Snide remarks;
Heavy-handedness.

O Cormac, Grandson of Conn," said Carbre,
"What is the worst argumentation?"
"That's easy," said Cormac:

Argumentation without learning, without
    knowledge;
Violence in discussion;
Discussion without reason.

Argumentation without consent,
without control,
without establishing anything,
without application.

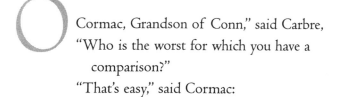

O Cormac, Grandson of Conn," said Carbre, "Who is the worst for which you have a comparison?"

"That's easy," said Cormac:

A man with the shamelessness of a lampooner,
with the contentiousness of a maid,

with the astuteness of a wily dog,
with the conscience of a dog,

with the hand of a thief,
with the strength of a bull,

with the discrimination of a lawyer,
with ingenious crafty intelligence,

with the speech of a prosperous man,
with the memory of a historian,

with the habits of an heir,
with the oath of a horse thief:
and he is shrewd, deceitful, hoary, vehement,
given to swearing, arrogant in saying, *It is
settled, I swear, I will take an oath.*

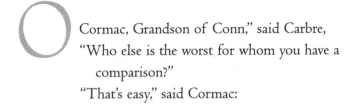 Cormac, Grandson of Conn," said Carbre,
"Who else is the worst for whom you have a
comparison?"
"That's easy," said Cormac:

A man who is harsh, bitter, uncouth;
violent, hasty, vulgar;
wild, forgetful, vociferous;
audacious, wise after the fact;

whom no one waits for and who waits for no
one;
who doesn't care what anyone says, and no one
cares what he says;
and he is shunned by tribe and church.

O Cormac, Grandson of Conn," said Carbre,
"I wish to know how I should be among the
smart and the stupid, among friends and
strangers, among the old and the young,
among the learned and the ignorant."
"That's easy," said Cormac:

Don't be too smart, don't be too stupid;
Don't be too proud, don't be too timid;
Don't be too haughty, don't be too humble;
Don't be too talkative, don't be too silent;
Don't be too hard, don't be too soft.

If you are too smart, expectations will be
imposed on you;
If you are too stupid, you will be duped.

If you are too proud, you will be shown
displeasure;
If you are too humble, you will be without
dignity.

If you are too talkative, you will be
inconsequential;
If you are too silent, you will be disregarded.

41

If you are too hard, you will be broken;
If you are too soft, you will be squashed.

A question," said Carbre: "How should I be?"
"That's easy," said Cormac:

Be intelligent to the intelligent,
so no one may dupe you by means of
    intelligence.

Be proud to the proud,
so no one may be over you causing you to
    quiver.

Be humble to the humble,
so your will may be done.

Be talkative to the talkative,
so you may be respected.

Be silent with the silent
when listening to information.

Be hard to the hard,
so no one treats you with contempt.

Be soft with the soft,
so everyone doesn't attack.

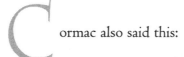

ormac also said this:

One is intelligent until one sells one's
   inheritance.
One is foolish until one acquires land.

One is a friend until it comes to debt.
One is a judge until it comes to children.

One is slothful until getting married.
One is virile until becoming religious.

One is respected until being defeated.
One is hospitable until refusing.

One is a nomad until homesteading.
One is a servant until one resides in one's own
   abode.

One is sound of mind until becoming drunk.
One is sensible until getting enraged.

One is well-behaved until committing sexual
   misconduct.
One is calm until fostering children.

One is confident until quarreling.

One is free until being denounced.

One is cheerful until misfortune occurs.
One is bold until refused.

One is a pedestrian until one is a charioteer.
All music is noble through the harp.

One who is prosperous is dignified.
One who is wretched is unseemly.

The sweetest sleep is lying together.
The sweetest ale is the first drink.

The sweetest music is music in the dark.
The sweetest person is the worthy one.

A young person who is tractable, humble,
    obedient, earnest in conscience and
    confession, will be beloved in youth,
    esteemed in old age, true in his word, noble
    in his appearance, high even if lowly, mature
    though youthful; his destiny with God and
    humanity will be good.

O Cormac, Grandson of Conn," said Carbre,
"What is the basis of ridicule among the
 Irish?"
"That's easy," said Cormac:

A man who is arrogant
on account of intelligence,
on account of gifts,
on account of fortune.

A man who is dressy, proud, slack.
A man who is lazy, irascible, weak, inclined to
 flight.
A man who is silly, stupid, boastful.

A man who is violent, aggressive, overbearing.
A man who is stingy, unreliable, jealous,
corrupt, fearful, touchy,
hasty, incautious, uncaring,
warlike, excessive, demanding.

O Cormac, Grandson of Conn," said Carbre,
"Who is the worst protector?"
"That's easy," said Cormac: "A protector of
little dignity who sells his honor, his
support, his hand, his breast, his heart, the
right of his clan, his people, and his
prowess."

His response is bare,
His compensation is empty.

His personality is speedy,
His amity is short-lived.

His protection is meager,
His reach is longer than his honor.

He is the image of a despised laughingstock to
all people;
He is ridiculous, unable to raise his head
wherever he may go or be.

S on, if you hearken to me," said Cormac, "this
is my counsel to you."

Don't let a man with followers be your
administrator.
Don't let a woman with sons and foster sons
be your manager.
Don't let a covetous man be your butler.
Don't let a man who procrastinates be your
miller.

Don't let an irascible, foul-mouthed man be
your envoy.
Don't let a lazy, complaining man be your
attendant.
Don't let a talkative man be your confidant.

Don't let a drunkard be your cupbearer.
Don't let a man with bad eyes be your
watchman.
Don't let a disagreeable, arrogant man be your
doorkeeper.

Don't let an indulgent man be your judge.
Don't let a man without knowledge be your
leader.

Don't let an unlucky man be your chief
advisor.

O Cormac, Grandson of Conn," said Carbre,
"Whom do you consider deaf, of what you've
heard?"
"That's easy—"

A doomed man being given a warning,
Someone being asked something he doesn't
like,
The gossip of a stupid woman.

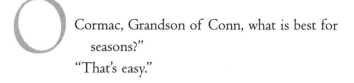

O Cormac, Grandson of Conn, what is best for
    seasons?"
"That's easy."

Winter fine and frosty,
Spring dry and breezy,
Summer dry with showers,
Autumn dewy and fruitful.

XXXVI

O Cormac, Grandson of Conn, what do you
    consider the worst you've heard?"
"That's easy."

A cry after calamity,
A groan of pain,
A womanish quarrel between two men.